New Rural Higher Education

About the Author

Prof. Ganapathy Palanithurai, Rajiv Gandhi Chair for Panchayati Raj studies, Department of Political Science and Development Administration, Gandhigram Rural Institute–Deemed University, Gandhigram is an academic activist working with academic community, civil society, policy community and political community to impress upon them the importance and need of democratic local governance in India to enable the poor to lead a decent dignified human life. All his academic, research and outreach activities are being supported by an array of funding agencies namely the World Bank, the UNDP, the UNICEF, the Hunger Project, SDC, DANIDA, Action Aid International, the Ford Foundation, Population Foundation of India, the Rajiv Gandhi Foundation, Toolkit Foundation–Netherland, Ministry of Panchayati Raj and State Planning Commission. He was a visiting Professor in Cologne University, Germany. He has to his credit seventy three books, 126 research articles, 112 popular articles in popular newspapers, 83 monographs published in a span of three decades. He is the coordinator of UGC-SAP and UGC innovative programme. He held several administrative positions like Dean, Faculty of Social Sciences, Dean, Student's Welfare, Member, Syndicate, Member Senate, Member, and Academic Council in Gandhigram Rural Institute. He was and is member of many advisory committees of the Government of India and Government of Tamil Nadu pertinent to local government and rural development.

New Rural Higher Education

Need of the Hour to Transform Rural India

G. PALANITHURAI

CONCEPT PUBLISHING COMPANY PVT. LTD.
NEW DELHI-110059

ISBN-13: 978-93-86682-68-0

First Published 2018

Published and Printed by

Concept Since 1974

Concept Publishing Company Pvt. Ltd.
A/15-16, Commercial Block, Mohan Garden,
New Delhi-110059 (INDIA)
T : 91 11 25351460, 91 11 25351794
E : publishing@conceptpub.com; *W* : www.conceptpub.com

Cataloging in Publication Data--Courtesy: D.K. Agencies (P) Ltd. <docinfo@dkagencies.com>

Palanithurai, G., author.
New rural higher education : need of the hour to transform rural India / G. Palanithurai.
pages cm
Includes bibliographical references and index.
Contents: Functioning of the rural institutes in India : a critical analysis / G. Palanithurai -- Vision for a National Rural University / V. Ragupathy.
ISBN 9789386682680

1. Education, Rural--India. 2. Education, Higher--Aims and objectives--India. 3. Gandhigram Rural Institute. I. Ragupathy, Varadarajan, 1958- Vision for a National Rural University. II. Title.

LCC LC5148.I5P35 2018 DDC 370.917340954 23

To

Divine Mother

Preface

Ever since I joined in the Gandhigram Rural Institute, I have tried to understand the purpose of the creation of the rural institute through literature, activities of the institute and the senior faculty members. What is the difference between the Rural Institute and Conventional Universities? What is the difference between the Rural Institute and Rural Development Institute? What are all the key characteristics of the Rural Institute? What are all the non-negotiable activities of the institute? are some the questions which I asked with the senior faculty members who were recruited by the founders of the rural institute. Further, I have read the writings of the founding fathers and mothers of the institute. I have gone through the annual reports of the institute in the formative years. While reading all the valuable documents I felt that the rural institute was created for a noble purpose. To understand the framework of the rural institute and to operationalise the framework of the institute, more number of visionaries, and committed faculty members are needed. In reality at the dawn of the institute, the teachers who joined with the founding father (Dr. G. Ramachandran) and mother (Dr. Soundaram Ramachandran) were the dedicated individuals who toiled and moiled for the effective functioning of the institute. They did not have proper salary and facilities and yet with a sense of commitment, they did dedicated services in the rural areas. In the beginning, the Gandhigram Rural Institute did only extension services and later started academic programmes. When it became a deemed university in 1976, the institute started moving towards the pattern of conventional higher learning institution by following their structure and functional norms and it became a government funded deemed university under the control of UGC. Here, it is to be underlined that its departure towards conventional university and not because of the UGC. The UGC has provided enormous scope for innovation and contextualisation through autonomy. It became more problematic to keep the framework of the government on the one hand and contextualising the institute on the other hand. I have been noticing the phenomenal growth of the institute and it catered to the needs of the rural populace and yet it could not retain the fundamentals of the Rural Institute because of the massive expansion of the institute. In this process, the institute acquired the characteristics of the conventional university. There are many factors contributed to the erosion of the values of the rural institute. But, new conditions of the rural areas need money more rural institutes to transform the rural communities and more particularly the rustic folk. People in the rural areas are in deep crisis and despite the implementation of plethora of schemes, the rural crises are acute. It is not mere an economic crisis and it is more than that. It is a crisis of rural values, culture and practices. In the era of globalisation, basic foundations of the village culture have been dismantled. To restore the rich values and transform the rural communities India needs new education for rural development and rural communities need new rural higher learning institutions called rural institutes. To restore the values and to contextualise the institute, the rural institute needs transformational leaders both at the helm of affairs and at the faculty level. Against this background, I have started investigating the reality and explaining the possibility of creating a new one or contextualising the old institute. The present volume is the outcome of the investigation that I have done in the past two decades. In this journey, Prof. V. Ragupathy joined with me to carve out a new framework for totally a new National Rural University. He has elaborated my basic framework for a new Rural Institute.

Acknowledgements

I have been obsessed with the operationalisation of the Rural Institute concept ever since I joined the institute in 1991 as I was committed passionately on the values of the rural institute. In this process I have earned the wrath of many both at the leadership level and at faculty level. When I joined with hope, passion, excitement, and commitment to work with community through educational programme. I have tried to understand the concept and I tried to do something at our level. Yet, my discourse continued and my obsession also continued as deviation from the main path of the Rural Institute continued day by day. In my discourse a large number of people participated and contributed. In fact, they have educated me and enlightened me which became a factor for my continued obsession. The discourse participants were and are many from different walks of life. Most of them are Gandhian leaders and civil society leaders. They are: Late V. Padmanabhan, Former Managing Trustee of Gandhigram; Late Dr. Aram, Former Vice-Chancellor; Dr. N. Markandan, Former Vice-Chancellor; Dr. T. Karunakaran, Former Vice-Chancellor; Late Dr. S. Narayanasamy, Head, Department of Gandhian Thought and Peace Science; Dr. V. Ragupathy my colleague working with me, Dr. M. Velusamy and Dr. A. Suriakanthi, Former Faculty Members of Gandhigram Rural Institute. They all gave their input on the essentials of Gandhian framework of education. Since all worked in the institute, they have indicated the reasons for this institute moving away from the main path of Gandhian framework. Moving towards conventional university is obvious and most do not want contextualising the same as Rural Institute. Because, it involves a prolonged struggle and teachers have to work hard in an adventurous way. They have to face challenges. No doubt, all challenges are opportunities but teachers do not proper orientation to take on the challenges and find solutions through their responses. Yet, the demand for a rural institute is always on the card to solve many of the rural problems at present. We at our level in the department performed our task within the framework of the Rural Institute. We struggled to influence others at a limited level within our institute selectively. Many of the occasions we are made answerable to the critiques of the Rural Institute. Our journey is not ending here. We want a new National Rural University to evolve educational programmes to transform the communities in the rural areas. We will pursue the same further. Our plea is not to upgrade our institute but to contextualise the institute to serve the rustic folk in the rural areas. I have been writing to insist that we need a Rural Institute. Our idea has been strengthened by a variety of stakeholders. I thank profusely all those who contributed richly for our thought process. I thank all our colleagues and family members for their unflinching support to our academic endeavours.

Contents

Introduction

The whole argument of rejuvenating the Rural Institute stems not from the perspective of the upliftment of the Rural Institute to a higher grade for the betterment of the staff of the institute but from the perspective of the conditions of the rural areas and the rural communities in India at present. At the dawn of Independence M.K. Gandhi had evolved a new framework of education to transform India more specifically the rural India as the villages were in rustic conditions. It is to be noted that India lives in villages. Indian culture basically evolves from the villages. India is a communitarian society. To transform rural India, M.K. Gandhi evolved a framework of education which is totally different from the educational system introduced by the British Administration. Gandhian framework of Education (*Nai Talim*) was also allowed to be practiced in India after Independence by the Central and State Governments. Having expanded the Western system of education, it has eaten away the new experiment of rural higher education advocated by M.K. Gandhi started at the dawn of Independence. But, one institute – the Gandhigram Rural Institute—continued to claim that it is a Rural Institute and got elevated to the level of a deemed university by keeping some of the values and symbols of the Rural Institute. For about three decades, this new experiment done by the Gandhigram Rural Institute had drawn the attention of global and national leaders. In the process of expansion and growth of the institute, the Rural Institute has started losing even the symbols and values nurtured over a period of time. The external agencies which have assessed and evaluated over a period of time made observation that the institute has moved slowly away from the basic objectives of the institute. Many observed that it is to be contextualised and the institute has to serve the rural communities. It is not only to work with the communities but also to work with civil society organisations and the government institutions. Totally it has to work for rural transformation by adopting the framework of M.K. Gandhi. It is a Gandhian Rural Transformation Institute. Beyond the above, the institute has got a greater role in shaping the policies of the government. Over a period of time, the Rural Institute is growing with the support of the UGC yet moved away unconsciously from the non-negotiable works. Having realised the drift the Institute tried its level best to do course correction.

Internally a few committees have been constituted to assess and evaluate the Institute from the perspectives of the objectives of the institute and the committees have made their own observations. But, many of the core recommendations of the committees have not been implemented. Here, it is necessary to make a mention that the external agencies which have evaluated the performance of the institute, have appreciated the hard work done by the staff in terms of the output the Institute has achieved by comparing the performance of the Institute with the performance of the conventional universities. But, while looking at the performance from the perspective of the objectives of the Rural Institute, they made all the remarks. Internally many staff members were self critical and they also indicated the lapses critically while looking at the overall functioning of the Institute. The institute leaders have been taking continuous efforts to orient the staff in the cultural moorings of the Rural Institute. But those orientations have not produced intended results.

In the globalisation context, all the efforts taken by the institute have not yielded any result in reorienting the institute as Neo-Rural Institute, as the institute has to follow national pattern of evaluation, assessment, organising courses and programmes on par with other universities with an aim of preparing the students for global and national labour market competitively. In order to get the recognisition and funds, there is no way to deviate from the main framework of education conceptualised by the government. But, occasionally some of the hard core committed faculty members used to ponder over the characteristics of the Rural Institute. The deviation has been indicated by many of the Gandhians and Gandhian institutions. Having gone to the fold of the Central Government for the sake of funds, there is no way to move away from mainstream framework of education. Since many of our teaching faculty involved in soul searching exercises, we do remember all those values through organising seminars, workshops and conferences but we could not move on as decided because our dancing to the tune of the funding agency. Compliance to the funding and regulatory agencies is far more important than moving in the path of Rural Institute. Apart from the above we conduct capacity building exercises for rural development personnels periodically. The students are exposed to rural institute values. But, they never internalise those values as the programmes of orientations are vague and weak. Students are passing out every year and the attributes, if they are checked with the students, one will find a great disappointment. With 150 teachers, more than 3500 students are being managed. Is it humanly possible to orient 3500 students by 156 teachers in the Gandhian values?

When Rural Institute began its work, more number of passionate individuals committed on the values of the rural institute joined without any expectations from the Institute. In order to develop the Institute, they personally suffered. With minimum pay and benefits, they richly contributed to the Institute through their hard work. All the activities are carried out by all both students and the staff. It was residential in nature. There was no salary structure, no hierarchy and all are committed workers. It was a community which runs the entire programme and activities. Their dedication, passion and commitment had been seen in the activities of the institute which drew the attention of the galaxy of leaders and intellectuals of the country and abroad. They pinned their hopes of the system which it has developed through their activities in the Rural Institute. All the leaders have registered their messages after visiting the activities of the institute in the visitor's book of the Institute. Those observations and remarks of the leaders could be compared with the observations and remarks of the review committee of the funding and ranking agencies.

The decline started only after the introduction of globalisation and more specifically after the appointment of individuals without having any background of Gandhian idea of education and Rural Institute as leaders of the Institute. Adoption of positions as followed in conventional universities has damaged the very functioning of the rural institute. One cannot accuse those individuals who run the administration and provided leadership, because they were chosen only by the Central Government. The officials of the Central Government have no perspective to look at the Rural Institute. Now, it is in a dilemma. It moved closer to the conventional university and deviated from the Rural Institute concept. At the dawn of globalisation in India, then Prime Minister Narasimha Rao had realised need of rural institutes and hence, he created a body called National Council for Rural Institutes (NCRI) in Hyderabad to create more number of Rural Institutes in the lines of the Gandhigram Rural Institute. He indicated it in his speech in the parliament during the creation of NCRI. But, unfortunately the NCRI has not taken shape and it was weakened and finally, it provided livelihood opportunity for a few. In this backdrop we looked at the rural crises and the education sector. Both are growing exponentially. Against this background, we are looking at both and we have come to a conclusion that to solve rural problems created through globalisation a new educational programme is needed. That could be given not by this institute in the present form. Hence, it is proposed a new National University. Rural crises could be tackled by the newly proposed National University with a new vision and strategies. This new venture should follow a new pattern and with a new structure totally new to the existing bureaucratic structure of the conventional universities. It should provide opportunity for the passionate people to work in this university. This monograph has two parts. One, critical analysis of the functioning of the rural institute, second one is the new proposal for the establishment of a National Rural University.

■ ■ ■

1

Functioning of the Rural Institutes in India: A Critical Analysis

G. *Palanithurai*

> "I claim to be a simple individual liable to err like any other fellow mortal. I own, however, that I have humility enough in me to confess my errors and to retrace my steps."
>
> **—M.K. Gandhi**

I am in the Gandhigram Rural Institute since April 1991. But, I was not brought up in Gandhian way of life and equally I was not oriented in Gandhian values through education. I studied in a conventional university and joined this institute with a passion that it is a different institute with unique characteristics. I have oriented myself in the culture of Gandhigram Rural Institute and carved out my own programmes and activities. But, I realised the fact that unless the institutions are contextualised and reoriented to the need of the society, the institutions will fade away losing engagement with the earlier vision and hence I have continuously worked for strengthening grassroots institutions and democracy. From that perspective I have looked at the functioning of the Gandhigram Rural Institute in the larger backdrop of the Rural Institutes in India. I have been in many of the core institutional governance responsibilities apart from designing academic, research and outreach activities of my own department. The critical remarks which I have made in this article are not with an objective of accusing anyone but with a hope of correcting ourselves to realise the objectives fixed by the founding fathers and mothers of the Rural Institutes in India. Against his backdrop, the article has to be read. I may be excused if there is any element of bias in my argument due to my personal attachment with the concept of "Rural Institute".

Introduction

The challenges before the governing institutions in India both at the Centre and State are from the rural areas as 68 per cent of the people still are living in the villages. Their life and livelihood conditions are being disturbed by the reckless exploitation of the natural resources by the efforts of the state and the market to achieve economic growth and development. Fast urbanisation that takes place in India at the cost of the villages. People in the villages more particularly the poor are in vulnerable conditions. Indian villages are virtually facing a crisis of existence. The intellectual community is not able to understand perspectively and address the problems of the people in the rural areas. Our higher learning institutions are untouched by the sufferings of the rural masses. Hence, the higher learning institutions' priorities are based on the needs of the market and the industries. People in the rural areas have been reduced into beneficiaries or petitioners or voters and beyond it, they are not considered as responsible citizens of this country despite they have constitutional rights and duties. Farming communities, tribal communities, craft communities, nomads, part of fishing communities in the rural areas constitute majority in India. They are the real faces of India. India's identity comes only from them. Yet, they are marginalised and a few segments in the rural areas are totally vulnerable and as a result their livelihood conditions are in deplorable conditions. People who live in the rural areas are weakened and disempowered. They are in total distress and the institutions and organisations created for upliftment of the rural poor have been dismantled functionally as villages are under the regulations of more than thirty seven departments of the government. Village life has been conditioned and regulated yet they could not lead a decent, dignified, joyful human life with full potentials and with the support of science and technology. The existing conditions in the villages are the outcome of the development activities initiated by the governments to achieve economic growth through industrial, service and knowledge economy over a period of time.

The exploitation of the natural resources is further intensified in the era of globalisation.[1] Inequality among the human collectivities is deeply widened. This has been done through an educational process which helped only the urban sector by neglecting the rural areas. In the seventy years of rural development activities in India governments have implemented more than 2000 schemes and programmes in the rural areas[2] and yet, they have not enabled the rural populace to lead a decent and dignified human life. Majority in the rural areas are neglected and marginalised. Against this background, sensible academics and policy makers lamented that the present educational system is helpful only to a few segments and leave a larger segment of the society unattended and susceptible to exploitation. They made a plea for revival of rural higher education which was introduced at the dawn of independence based on the Gandhian Framework of Education and Development.[3] It is in this context, an attempt is made to analyse the functioning of the Rural Institutes which had been initiated at the dawn of independence to experiment Gandhian Framework of Education and through which transformation could be achieved in Indian villages. It is a major question, whether the rural institutions created as per the vision of Gandhi on Education have created any significant impact in the rural areas as expected. Have the Rural Institutes drawn the attention of the policy community through their impact making performance? It is being undertaken with a aim of doing policy advocacy to the Government of India at present to revamp the whole educational system with the perspective of enabling the rural masses to transform themselves to lead a decent dignified human life. Before embarking into an analysis of the functioning of the Rural Institutes one has to have a conceptual clarity on the concept "Rural Institute or Rural University".

Framework on Rural Institutes

'Rural Institute' and 'Rural University'[4] had been in discourse and operation along with the mainstream higher education system for the past seventy years in India. Though, ideally the concepts had been spoken, the Rural Institute system had not been widely recognised and strengthened as a system of higher education in India despite many such institutes were created at the dawn of independence to experiment Gandhi's Framework of Education. It is to be noted that all the institutions though followed the framework of education of M.K. Gandhi, are not prototype in their functioning. Each one was distinct as they were conceptualised by the Gandhians as they were the architects of the institutions.[5]

To concept 'Rural Institute' had been interpreted differently by the scholars and administrators. Now it has been reduced as a Non-Governmental Organisation from the perspective of National Council of Rural Institutes (NCRI).[6] Being an academic working in a Rural Institute for about 20 years I could make out the nature of confusion from the level of the head of the institution to the last person working in the institute. Only a few academics understood and they too are not able to operationalise the concept into reality in their domain of activities. Some argue that Rural Institute is meant for achieving rural development and many perceive that it is meant for educating the rural poor boys and girls. A few argue that it is nothing but preparing human power for rural development activities of the government agencies and civil society organisations. Yet, Gandhians argue that it is the development of the post basic education conceptualised based on the Gandhian Framework of Education.[7] It is a new kind of exercise to evolve alternative model of education to achieve alternative development.[8] Rural Institutes have to prepare human power for achieving rural transformation through Gandhian perspective. At present many do not know what is Rural University or Rural Institute and what for it was created? To get clarity one has to trace from authentic source. In my opinion we have to trace the concept and explanation from the writings and speeches of the founders of the Rural Institute.

No doubt (Rural University System) is not a system adopted or adapted from any other system outside India. It is indigenous in origin. It is in Indian tradition of educational system. India has its own rich knowledge tradition. No civilisation can flourish without a knowledge base. Wide references are available for *Gurukula* system, the great hermitage of scholars and philosophers functioning in India. In the same way world renowned universities like those of Nalanda and Taxila functioned in Indian region. These institutions drew scholars from all over the world. The Rural University system which we talk about was in the blood and bone of the history of India. Our culture and civilisation rooted in the rural life of the people. All our activities were around the villages. It was only during the British period the rural areas were more and more neglected and attention was paid only to a few hundred towns and cities. Since a few development activities were initiated in the urban areas, people in the rural areas started migrating to urban centres. When higher education institutions were created in a few towns and cities, people who know the implications of higher education moved out of the rural areas only with a specific purpose of educating their children in the urban centres. As a result rural masses were totally neglected and kept far away from the reach of higher education.

Though millions of the people were having aspiration to enjoy higher education they were compelled to remain in the rural areas as their livelihood depended on agriculture. They were not able to migrate from the rural areas. In order to cater to the needs of the rural masses, an education system was needed that too in the rural area itself and that too without affecting their livelihood and their rural activities. Nowhere, it was in the thought process of the leaders and opinion markers. It was only a few Gandhian workers based on the system evolved by M.K. Gandhi reacted to the mainstream system of education imported, introduced and practiced in India by the British and subsequently it was followed by our Political *pandits*.

There were bold initiatives like Gurukula University at Haridwar created by Arya Samajists, the Visva Bharati University at Santiniketan established by the great poet and philosopher Rabindranath Tagore, the National University at Adayar established by Dr. Annie Besant. There was yet another path-breaking event, namely establishing Vidya Peeths of Gujarat and Bihar and subsequently Jamia Millia of Dr. Zakir Hussain. Attempts were there in history to provide an alternative system of education to the British system of education in India.[9]

'Rural University' or 'Rural Institute' was fundamentally an operational concept (to be debated) which gained currency among the policy makers and Gandhian academics for some time in India after the submission of the report of the University Education Commission under the chairmanship of Dr. Sarvepalli Radhakrishnan.[10] The Dr. Radhakrishnan Committee Report is one of the acclaimed reports in India in terms of its vision. In this report a chapter on 'Rural University' was incorporated. It was written by one of the Commission members Dr. Arthor E. Morgan, the President of the Tennessee River Valley Authority in the USA. He visualised an ideal university suited to Indian ethos. It is yet another paradox that a foreigner was able to show us the way. In this chapter an argument was advanced that the existing universities, focused on cities and towns and not on villages and the whole educational system was devised to prepare personnel for government jobs and not for social transformation. Morgan urged that India needed a different, distinct, independent institution to prepare cadre of leaders to bring about transformation in the Indian Rural society.[11] For three years from the advent of Independence it was only a concept in the making till Nanabhai Bhatt translated the idea of the Rural Institute into action in 1951 in Gujarat. In his preface to the booklet entitled "Gram Vidhyapith" he dwelt upon the foundation of the Rural University. According to him, the edifice of the Rural University should be built on '*Nai Talim*', the basic principle enunciated by Gandhiji. Bhatt unequivocally stated that the existing university culture had not shaped the younger generation with character, humility, commitment, responsibility and spirituality which was necessary to reconstruct the Indian society. It was to be recognised that the dreams of the founding fathers would be realised not through a few government servants and a few development schemes of the government, but only by invoking and involving the masses, for which a cadre of leaders and volunteers with a sense of commitment and values was needed.

Morgan's chapter on Rural Institutes has eight sections. In the first section he explains the context in which 'Rural Institutes' are visualised. The conditions of the villages and the basic education programme are explained. Undoubtedly, it is all based on the Gandhian Framework of Rural Reconstruction. India being a primarily rural society, has to be reconstructed in such a manner that the development achieved should be sustainable. The whole vision was against the on-going development process of modernisation, industrialisation, and Westernisation. It was to be almost a turning point in history.

In the second section post-basic education is explained. The third section deals with rural industrialisation. The fourth section explains the reconstruction of Indian villages. The fifth section is the core area which deals with the establishment of Rural Colleges and Universities. In this section the characteristics, the curriculum and the methodology are explained. The sixth section deals with the basic concerns of Rural Universities. What kind of management and administrative systems have to be developed to manage the rural educational institutions, is explained. The final section sum up the whole argument. The whole chapter challenges Gandhian educationists to conceptualise new education programmes which are to be integrated with the entire education system and policies of the government. It is to be noted here that the mainstream education system followed the model of the West. The British system of education had taken roots in Indian soil and was in vogue. For the new system of education every aspect had to be worked out and to be integrated with the existing system so that it could be acceptable to policy makers for evolving policies and allocating resources for strengthening the new educational system. As per this chapter, if the new framework for establishment of Rural Higher Education Institutions raised hopes among policy makers, the entire education system would be totally oriented towards the Gandhian framework.

In 1954 the Government of India appointed a committee under the chairmanship of Dr. K.L. Shrimali to look into higher rural education and offer recommendations. The above Committee submitted its report and suggested an umbrella institutional set-up to coordinate the Rural Institutes' academic activities. Based on the recommendation of the Shrimali Committee the National Council for Rural Higher Education (NCRHE) was established in 1955. In the first phase the National Council for Rural Higher Education identified ten institutions called "Rural Institutes" which would be later developed into rural universities. The ten institutions were:

1. Shri Niketan (West Bengal)
2. Jamia Millia Islamia (New Delhi)
3. Mouni Vidhyapith (Gargoti, Kolhapur)
4. Shivaji Lok Vidyapith (Amravati)
5. Gandhigram (Madurai)
6. Vidyabhawan (Udaipur)
7. Ramakrishna Mission Vidyalaya (Coimbatore)
8. Lok Bharti (Sanosara, Saurashtra)
9. Toorki (Bihar)
10. Balwani Vidyapith (Bichpuri, Agra)

Of them the Gandhigram Rural Institute is one.

The Gandhian Rural Institute was created in the year 1956 by its parent body Gandhigram Trust. The Trust was founded by Dr. Soundaram and Dr. G. Ramachandran as Gandhigram Society on 7th August, 1947. The Gandhigram Trust have several units and institutions to work for rural transformation. From 1947 to 1956 many institutions have been developed. Of which one is the Gandhigram Rural Institute. It started with outreach programmes and later moved over to organising academic programmes. Only at a later stage, after it became a deemed university it started research activities. Its aim was to transform the rural communities to lead a decent scientific human life with dignity. It tried to provide needed knowledge, service, human power, technology to the rural areas. The academic programmes were basically organised through work with the communities. It devoted its attention on livelihood, sanitation, rural industries, poverty reduction, and social transformation through its continuous committed work. Jawaharlal Nehru, Dr. Rajendra Prasad, Martin Luther King from the USA visited the institute and registered their observations about the functioning of this Rural Institute. After seeing the activities of the institute, the status of the institute had been changed from Rural Institute to a deemed university in the year 1976 fully funded by the Government of India through the University Grants Commission. While changing the status into a Deemed University, it could not evolve a unique governance system by following the Gandhian principles but it tried to follow the traditional university to suit the requirements of the funding agency, the UGC. It was a tightrope walk for the Deemed University to keep the balance between the academic programmes in line with conventional university and outreach programmes in line with Rural Institutes. Teaching learning methods and academic programmes have been designed in such a way that the students coming out from this Institute go for higher education, and job as other students coming out from traditional universities. Despite all trials and tribulations it tried its best to retain the characteristics of the Rural Institute. At that point of time it was well appreciated. Even at that point, a distinct structure could have been created suitable to the Rural Institutes' objectives. Instead the Gandhigram Rural Institute opted to follow the model of the conventional universities. This prompted the Gandhigram Rural Institute to make a slow departure from the basic characteristics of the Rural Institute.

The courses offered in the beginning were changed by citing the reasons stated by earlier Rural Institutes and, gradually, barring a few, all the degrees up to the masters came to be modelled on those of the traditional universities. The appointment of the Vice-Chancellor has played a crucial role in deciding the fate of the Rural Institutes. On many occasions Vice-Chancellors were appointed without any Rural Institute background. They managed the Institute to suit their own philosophy. Teachers recruited to this Institute have not been oriented rigourously to change their attitude and behaviour. As a result the institutions were caught in the dilemma of either to go back to a 'Rural Institute' character or transform into a conventional university which they really could not do. It does not mean the delivery of the institute is weak. The Institute has faculty with capacity and commitment delivered services in academic, outreach and research programmes more in terms of quantity and quality when it is compared to the traditional universities. It is evident from the ranking of the institute by the NAAC.[12] One has to understand the challenges for the Rural Institutes had to be faced by the leaders of the Institutes by their innovative and committed action. They needed the support of the Government. In this context it is necessary to recognise and assess the honest attempts made by different institutions.

Box-I
Rural Institute: Characteristics

1. A rural university should be founded ideologically on the conviction that there are certain material, mental and spiritual values in the ancient rural civilisation and culture of India which require to be rediscovered and renourished and that not necessarily in conflict with the values of the scientific and technological developments in the modern world.
2. Among the values of a rural culture would be peacefulness of daily life in place of restlessness and the fret and the fury coming from such restlessness; cooperativeness and adjustments in place of competition and strife in the economic order; decentralisation of political and economic power and resources in order to reach out to hundreds of thousands of villages; the proper balancing of material and moral claims of life; and above all, a deeper and functioning artistry permeating the common life of the people. There will be no question of setting aside modern science or technology but their application on a more broad-based, human and humane manner will have to be truthfully accomplished.
3. A Rural University should take higher education to the doors of the people where they live close to the soil and with agriculture as their main occupation. Therefore, inevitably much of higher education in rural areas will be in and through agriculture.
4. Closely allied to agriculture would be the place of village industries and handicrafts. Rural Higher Education will thus be, in a measure at least, woven around village industries and handicrafts.
5. A Rural University should neither be too big nor centralised. It should be comparatively smaller than the urban university, but at the same time it should spread out its programme through extension methods.
6. A Rural University should depend more and more on local resources, both human and material, and aim at a large measure of self-sufficiency through the productive work of its own teachers and students.
7. Two languages at least will be compulsory, namely the mother tongue or regional language and Hindi, the national language. Any other language like English may be added to these two, but there should be no subtraction from these two.

(*Contd.*)

8. There should be no steam-rolling to produce identical patterns everywhere, but local colour, tones and traditions must be allowed to come in freely without losing certain general standards and attainments.
9. While providing for a measure of specialisation in techniques, a Rural University will aim at the development of integrated personality in men and women so that the future citizen will know how to lead a balanced life. The economic, social and spiritual claims must be reconciled in the character and outlook of the growing generation.
10. The Rural University must revitalise a whole rural area in which it is situated. Life inside the campus should illuminate and reflect itself fully in the increased education, prosperity and happiness of the people in the rural areas. That certainly would be a real test.

Source: G. Ramachandran "Rural Universities" in Gandhigram Rural Institute, *Gandhigram Rural Institute of Higher Education*. Gandhigram: Gandhigram Rural Institute, 1960, pp. 2-4.

Within a short span of time the Rural Institutes faced a plethora of problems because they were not in the broader framework of the Indian education system. In 1958, the problems of the Rural Institutes were discussed in an international seminar at Bichpuri. The Rural Institutes could not move further in the existing framework as they were caught in the bureaucratic net and, as a result, the Rural Institutes faced innumerable hurdles. Having experienced turbulent weather, the Rural Institutes had decided to be merged with the traditional university system within fifteen years of their existence without creating much impact and they turned towards the Western mode of educational system by changing into constituent colleges of affiliated universities.[13]

If an analysis is made as to why the Rural Institutes could not survive, one would meet with surprises. It is necessary to keep the basic objectives as referral points for evaluation. The objective was to create a cadre of rural development leaders and managers to tackle the problems of the rural communities. Programmes were to be offered not to seek employment opportunity in government departments. They would be real change makers to bring about rural transformation. But the main reason attributed for the failure was that the graduates who passed out of the Rural Institutes were not able to get admission to the traditional university system and appointments in government services. From these arguments one can infer easily that the students admitted to the Rural Institutes were not moulded, motivated, oriented and trained towards the objectives of the Rural Institutes. The students who got admitted to the Rural Institutes were also having the same objective of seeking jobs in the government system as the students in the traditional educational institutions.

The Gandhigram Rural Institute was the only institute that continued as a Rural Institute and delivered what it ought to deliver to the rural masses at a limited level with the dedicated staff under the leadership of Dr. G. Ramachandran. The staff who worked in the Rural Institute could not get remuneration as their counterparts elsewhere and yet they served the institute with a sense of commitment.

Assessment of the First Phase

Thus fourteen Rural Institutes (ten plus four) had been started in India at the dawn of Independence. These fourteen Rural Institutes supposed to offer alternative system of education in India based on the Gandhian Framework of Education. Unfortunatively, of the fourteen, one institute remained as rural higher education institute and all other institutions had transformed themselves to join with the mainstream system of education in India. The remaining one is also functioning neither as a Rural Institute nor as a full-fledged university. It tries to ape the traditional universities but it tries to keep certain values of the Rural Institute developed over a period of time. Now almost Rural Institute as a distinct category of educational institution based on the framework evolved for Rural Institutes in India is an extinct entity. But, there are many institutions carrying the label of rural institute but do not reflect the characteristics. They are both in the government fold and in the domain of Non-Governmental Organisations (NGOs).

Rural Higher Education gained momentum in Gujarat by the setting up of Gram Vidyapiths. Lok Bharti, though it remained an inspiring concept, could not leap forward despite the attempts made continuously. Three Gram Vidyapiths were established in Gujarat. They were in Bahadurpur (Baroda District), Samoda (Mehsana District) and Vedchi (Surat District). A Gram Vidyapith Society was formed to strengthen the initiatives of these Vidyapiths. To further their activities the Gujarat State Basic Education Board was sought to be established to coordinate the activities of '*Nai Talim*' right from Primary to Rural Higher Education. The proposal for establishing the Board statutorily failed miserably. The Rural Institutes created with enthusiasm, commitment and sincerity had not projected with a positive message to the policy makers and the people that the new scheme of education would deliver the goods and solve the problems of the rural communities.

The students who passed out of these institutions faced many problems as they were from totally a different stream from the mainstream framework of Higher Education in India. Many students from the Rural Institutes who wanted to pursue higher studies found it difficult to get admission to the conventional universities. Many who tried to get government jobs by showing the degree obtained from Rural Institutes could not get them. This has been projected as a reason for the drifting away from the concept of the 'Rural Institute'. This has been projected as the failure of the Rural Institutes. The real issue, however, is that the Rural Institutes had not performed as they ought to. In the name of Rural Institutes they performed the job of a college affiliated to a conventional university. It is also a paradox that these Rural Institutes which were expected to perform the unique role of Rural Institutes were brought under the rubric of the UGC. The UGC pattern is different and totally opposite to the direction of the Rural Institutes. In order to get funds, the Rural Institutes had to adhere to the norms of the UGC and, as a result, the Rural Institute experiments were diluted. Therefore, they could not register any visible impact. They could not improve sanitation or livelihood, protect rural industries, innovate appropriate technology, provide health facilities, literacy, and, work for social change. When Rural Institute was created it worked on all those critical issues of development as there were no institutional mechanism in the Government. But, now for all the issues, they have units in the government departments and specific schemes with officials. Hence, Rural Institute concentrates, on students production. Thus, Rural Institute exists in name and produce students through academic programmes. Beyond certain periods they could not continue as rural institute in spirit and hence they have been merged with the conventional institutions. The old institutions like the Gandhigram Rural Institute and the new ones like the Chitrakoot Institute struggled to survive as they did not have appropriate leadership excepting the Vice-Chancellors. They too were mere managers for three years to run the show. All the functional values and skills evolved at the time of the creation of the Rural Institute have been imparted through teaching mode mechanically as internalisation of such values for practices among the teaching staff is weak. As a result, those values are not in the attitudinal and behavioural traits of the students and the teachers. Yet, those values are in the system as symbols.[14] They could not improve the functioning substantially. They could not provide ideological leadership for the Rural Institute. But continuously steps have been taken to reposition the institute as Rural Institute[15]. But due to the liberal funding of the UGC, they improved the infrastructure and enabled the staff to improve their career. They could not come out with academic programmes which could foster skills needed for reconstructing the rural areas and transforming the rural landscape. Sometimes, to justify their distinctiveness, the Rural Institutes introduced courses and programmes with a rural bias but the students could not get gainful employment. It is a hard fact that the students, joining to the Rural Institutes are from the lowest level of performance in schools with very little motivation.

Rural Institutes are being viewed as non-profitable white elephants. Only students with a low academic profile and low motivation join the institutes. Further, the rural institutes are driven by the funding agencies to produce more number of students as do the colleges. Despite all constraints, the Rural Institute serves the poor in the rural areas through its academic, outreach and research programmes. This kind of drive completely pushes the Rural Institutes away from the traditional institutions of learning. Hence affiliating these Rural Institutes to the traditional university system was inevitable and imperative from the perspective of the students' future as they did not have the needed motivation and commitment to serve in the rural areas for rural reconstruction and transformation. Here one has to recognise and underline that Rural Institutes were created not to train students to get clerical positions in government offices. They were to become change agents in the rural areas. But, unfortunately, a perception was developed that the students who got degrees and diplomas have to go for higher studies or get employment opportunity in the government sector. When Rural Institutes were seen from that perspective, many felt that the students faced problems. Moreover, many wanted to move with the mainstream education rather than carve out a different path distinctively different from the mainstream educational system. Even the degrees and diplomas in Rural Institutes were designed to suit the requirements of the traditional colleges and universities. In the meanwhile, the schools preparing students through basic and post-basic education started disappearing. The Gandhian Institutions which had supported the Rural Institutes declined in terms of their activities in the framework of Gandhi. It is to be noted significantly that the Gandhigram Trust a vibrant Gandhian Organisation maintaining all its activities despite the challenges.[16] But, it is unfortunate the Gandhigram Rural Institute has severed its ties with the parent body which originally created this Rural

Institute. This transformation was due to the drive from the Government through its stipulation. It is a loss for the Institute. Thus the Rural Institutes gradually lost their original character, mandate, approach and activities. They were all merged or affiliated with the traditional university system. The freedom of Gandhian experiments was given the go-by. The Rural Institutes started functioning as a soft variant of the traditional colleges and universities. Thus, the Rural University or Rural Institute began to fade away. Only a few institutions have survived with lot of problems. Thus, the face of the rural university has been changed and it has assumed the characteristics of a college or a miniature traditional university.

New Initiatives

The concept of 'Rural University' gained much prominence after the release of the New Education Policy in the year 1986. It states that the new pattern of the rural university will be consolidated on the lines of Mahatma Gandhi's revolutionary ideas on education so as to take up the challenges of micro planning at the grassroots for the transformation of the rural areas for which institutions and programmes of Gandhian Basic Education will be supported. The policy envisages that educational institutions and voluntary agencies which take up educational programmes based on the concept of correlation between socially useful productive work, social service and academic study will be encouraged. Why did the New Education Policy reemphasise the need for the Rural Institute? It has to be viewed in perspective. Rural problems are mounting enormously and poverty reduction has become a real challenge to the rural development departments. Against this background the Central Government needed professional institutions to tackle the issues in the rural areas. Whether it was water supply, or sanitation, or livelihood, or primary education or primary health, or waste management, or rural energy, or rural employment the government required nodal institutions to help the government take appropriate policy decisions and implement them to achieve the targeted outcome. For this they needed institutions. Against this background the New Education Policy emphasized the need for rural higher education institutions. A Programme of Action was drawn up by the Ministry entitled New Education Policy 1986. It advocated:

(a) Consolidation of the existing rural universities;
(b) Reorganisation of the Rural Institutes established as a part of schemes of rural higher education launched in the Second Five Year Plan;
(c) Encouraging other institutions to take up Rural Reconstruction;
(d) Strengthening Rural Development Educational Programmes in select institutions;
(e) Supporting the elementary, secondary and post-basic institute based on '*Nai Talim*';
(f) Strengthening the content of all these institutions with emphasis on science and technology; and
(g) Setting up of National Rural Institutes Council to manage the affairs of Rural Institutes and Rural Universities.

Nothing moved beyond preparation of documents for about six years. This New Education Policy was modified in 1992 and, subsequently, based on the new recommendations, the National Council for Rural Institutions (NCRI) was established in 1995 at Hyderabad by the Government of India. It is a registered society fully funded by the Government of India.[17]

It is to be noted here that how the newly created NCRI was to function was underlined clearly in the inaugural speech of the then Prime Minster of India, P.V. Narasimha Rao, on 3rd December, 1995.[18] His whole argument was to contextualise the Rural Institutes: they have to create cadres to manage development programmes. The cadres coming out from Rural Institutes should not be job hunters but job creators. The Rural Universities have to act as catalysts to help the communities through ideas, knowledge, skills and technology. These institutions have to transform the unskilled individuals into skilled workers to meet the market needs. The village life situation has to be transformed by implementing the constructive programmes, the activities ranging from village sanitation, water supply, livelihood, literacy, skill upgradation, small industries, infrastructure, communication, credit system, panchayats act. The gap between the higher level government and the people has to be narrowed down. The Central Government evolves excellent policies, schemes and programmes. It allocates plenty of resources for rural development activities but they do not reach the field. The schemes and programmes evolved by the Central Government have to be implemented speedily and professionally for which the Rural Universities have to work continuously as facilitators. Appropriate technologies have to be developed in the Rural Institutes and they are to be disseminated and transferred to the communities. In China, two universities are helping rural artisans to prepare articles out of bamboo for export. In this way traditional universities are working in China to help the rural communities. The existing Rural Institutes in India have to rise to that level to lend their help to the rural community based on their experience.[19] To evolve new technologies and to upgrade the skills needed by the market are the imperative tasks of the Rural Institutes. In this manner it was emphatically stressed, the Rural Institutes are to be contextualised[20] in the market era.

The Rural Institutes have to act as a support base for rural communities to make use of the opportunities coming from economic globalisation and, at the same time, if there are threats from globalisation, they are to be tackled by the community through the new Panchayati Raj System. Such a kind of contextualisation has to be done in all Rural Universities.[21] Communities have to be in touch with the Rural Institutes for their needs. Such an interface has to be created between the Rural Institutes and the communities. A new cadre has to be created to manage the rural development programmes. These Rural Institutes are to be integrated with the larger society by which needed skills, capacity, technology and idea input will be provided. It was with this vision that the NCRI was created and, through a few Rural Universities was expected to function vibrantly. But now the question is how are they functioning and what have they achieved? These questions have to be answered objectively and honestly.

Assessment of the Second Phase

It is necessary to assess to what extent the second attempt to establish Rural Institutes and Universities has taken shape and to what extent the old Rural Institutes have lived up to their objectives. To be very frank, Rural Institutes were started but they could not survive and they disappeared. Only a few institutes are surviving. The NCRI was created only to rejuvenate the existing institutions and to establish new ones too. Hence, the assessment has to cover the NCRI and the old Rural Institutes surviving until now. First, one has to understand that rural development activities are facilitated not only by the Rural Institutes but also by many agencies in this country. There are government training institutions, specialised research institutes of higher order, departments (e.g. Rural Development) in traditional universities, civil society organisations continuously working for rural development by training the stakeholders involved in rural development activities, both leaders and officials, preparing needed cadres for rural development, assisting fieldwork or working as outsourcing units. They are not designated as rural academic bodies but they do work for rural transformation and rural reconstruction.

Even after sixty years of continuous rural development activities by several agencies with plenty of schemes and programmes and pumping of huge resources, we could not make a bold statement that conditions have been created in the rural areas to facilitate a decent human life with all basic facilities. It is self-evident from the point of view of human development. Despite our schemes, programmes and huge resources for rural development, we could not create much impact on human development. Where are we now, in the human development report? Our position in human development will reveal our real achievements and failures. Even smaller countries with less growth have gone up in human development. Ours is a huge country with vast differences and it has been managed centrally and not in a decentralised fashion. Till now we have developed a perception among the people that 'development' is the work of the government and not of the community. People have developed a dependency syndrome and consider and perceived themselves as beneficiaries and petitioners, not as development participants or citizens. To tackle all the problems of the people in the rural areas, governments, both Central and State, develop plans centrally and not in a decentralised way. But it is an irony that some of our districts are larger than some countries in the world. Even within a state one finds a vast difference between or among the districts. Even within a district one finds much difference among the blocks. Genuine and effective decisions are taken, programmes are evolved, but to operationalise the same in different regions and sub-regions, concrete action plans are needed locally. Generic decisions, policies, programmes and schemes are chalked out, but to dovetail them to the specific area, we need a specific action framework for implementation. Who will create such a plan at the district level and sub-district levels? The 74th Amendment to the Constitution of India says that it is mandatory on the part of every District Planning Committee to prepare a development plan for the whole of the district. But there is no district plan machinery barring in a few states.

India has got a vast human resource but they are not being used profitably. In the era of globalisation, for global products, markets are found even in remote villages. But to find a market for local products, there is no integrated system. As a result, cottage and village industries are ruined. Many traditional skills have disappeared. Village life is not self-reliant but is dependent. In this way villages have been transformed. In fact, villages have been deserted. All economic activities are city and town centric. Hence one finds large scale migration from villages to urban areas and urbanisation becomes rapid by the day. Economic growth has picked up. But living conditions in the rural areas are becoming difficult. The majority in the villages are living in sub-human living conditions. These are the reasons for our stagnation in the Human Development Index.

Three centuries ago India and China retained half of the wealth and riches in the world with half of the population in the world. Now India, though poised for 8 to 9 per cent growth, cannot proclaim that it has enabled the people to lead a decent and dignified human life.[22] Yet, 71 per cent of the population is living in the rural areas. Of them 58 per cent to 60 per cent rely on agriculture for their livelihood. Agriculture does not contribute substantially to economic growth and farmers have committed suicide due to crop failures and due to the vagaries of the monsoon. It results in large scale exodus of people to urban areas and it has made life in towns and cities miserable. The water level has gone down. Sanitation is poor in rural areas. Public schools have poor facilities and show ineffective functioning. Environmental degradation has set in. Skills in the rural areas have disappeared as they are not in demand. People have been reduced to beneficiaries and consumers rather than development participants. Still villages are in a feudal set-up as an agri-based economy is practiced and a hierarchical caste system plays a predominant role alongside patriarchy.

To bring about the needed change in the rural areas everyone looks to educational institutions. Why do we look to educational institutions for rural transformation despite the plethora of government programmes for rural development? For establishing effective linkage between the government and the communities we need catalyst institutions. The rural institutions can function as catalyst institutions. It does not mean that there are no higher educational institutions in the rural areas. There are many institutions in the rural areas, but they are prototype Engineering Colleges, Arts and Science Colleges, Paramedical Training Institutions and even Medical Colleges. They are all just located in the rural areas. But, there is absolutely no connection between the community and the educational institutions. Very near to the engineering colleges, villages are affected due to inadequate water supply and poor sanitation. This is not being attended to. It could be solved very easily by the intervention of the engineering colleges. Very near to medical colleges poor women and children are affected by anaemia and malnutrition. They could be attended to by the medical colleges. In reality they are not doing so. These educational institutions are modelled on the colonial pattern, which always commanded the intellectual resources of the people and never sought to educate the natives and draw out the best from them. The system excludes dalits, women and tribals. Further the structure of these educational institutions has not been democratised, but remain hierarchical, nurturing the feudal culture. They are not only feudal and exploitative but also patriarchal. The staff are career oriented. The do not connect themselves with the society in the absence of a mandate for outreach programmes. By overcoming all these problems, educational institutions have to be reorganised to meet the requirements of the community. It is to be recognised and understood that the educational institutions have a rich potential to be extended to the community.[23] But, unfortunately, we do not have an institutional mechanism to transfer the rich potential or extendables in the form of ideas, technologies and skills to the rural communities. Before the introduction of new Rural Institutes, the existing educational institutions have to find a way to reach out to the communities.[24]

In each and every college, a department can be created for outreach programmes as a special drive of the University Grants

Commission, by which systematic steps can be taken to conduct outreach programmes in the communities very near to a college or university. By doing so many of the issues and problems can be investigated by the academic institutions and, based on the findings, policy advocacy can be done by the same institutions. By doing all these activities, universities and colleges can establish effective linkages with the society. Thus even the traditional and conventional colleges and universities can reach out to the society systematically through an institutional mechanism. Then one can think about the establishment of Rural Institutes and Rural Universities.

The Rural Institutes were brought under the administrative system of the UGC, which is meant for conventional universities. The Rural Institutes which are in the ambit of the UGC have to move in the direction shown by the UGC. The leaders who are coming here for three years as Vice-Chancellors want to follow the guidelines of the UGC as it is the main funding agency instead of moving as per the objectives of the Rural Institutes. It is necessary that to manage the Rural Institutes, we identify persons with a deep understanding of the functioning of the Rural Institutes. But in reality, on many occasions, we cannot find persons with such a background to lead the Rural Institutes. Further the fundamental principles that shaped the edifice of the Rural Institute, the Gandhian framework, is yet another issue to be discussed. The whole Rural Institute concept is developed on the concept of "*Nai Talim*" of Gandhiji. The Rural Institutes came into being to cater to the needs of the students coming out from basic and post-basic education schemes. This amounted to developing a scheme of academic, research and extension activities on the principles of basic and post-basic education strongly rooted in '*Nai Talim*' of Gandhiji. When basic and post-basic educations were given a go-by how could Rural Institutes get students with such a background?

It is mandatory for the Rural Institutes to prepare the people for self rule and build the capacity of the people to participate in the development process. But, the development framework enunciated by Gandhiji has to be followed.[25] The Rural Institutes have been brought under the framework of institutions which are in the process of modernisation and industrialisation. Having realised the weakness of this move, the National Council for Rural Institutes was created to set right the Rural Institutes. But, the Rural Institutes were not brought under the domain of the NCRI. Thus NCRI became an entity like the ICSSR, the ICHR and other institutions to provide funding support to the institutes working on the objectives and programmes of the funding agencies. Though the NCRI was initially under the guidance of Dr. Aram, former Vice-Chancellor of Gandhigram Rural University, and later of Mr. L.C. Jain, a noted Gandhian, the NCRI was not placed on a sound ideological and financial footing. Both of them were highly respected Gandhians and recognised persons in the policy making bodies. When they were in the NCRI they were close to the government also. They could have impressed upon the policy makers the need of strengthening of the NCRI and bringing the Rural Institutes under the ambit of the NCRI. Both of them struggled with the bureaucrats even for the normal functioning of the NCRI. As a result the NCRI emerged as a funding agency to sponsor some of the activities of the institutions which are well within the Gandhian framework of activities. That is why the officials are asking why we need the NCRI to fund educational institutions and NGOs as we have the UGC and the Rural Development Ministry to fund these institutions respectively. We could not create a set of institutions which are well within the framework of the NCRI.

The Central Government has declared that it would create world class management institutes, technology institutes, science institutes, central universities and so on. There is no mention about world class Rural Institutes to prepare cadres for rural development activities. Policy makers concentrate more on economic growth and human resource development in cities and towns and forget about the well-being of the people who are in the rural areas. Rural reconstruction and rural transformation need a totally different governance system, administrative system, livelihood system, economic system, credit system for which a new set of cadres are needed. An organic interaction is needed between the academy and the communities. Gandhiji framed an ideal village system and this will be a referral point. This ideal village system has its own value framework. Keeping this in mind, the university has to work for it. One should not assume that the interaction between the institute and the community is free. There is the state, which takes up the responsibility of bringing development to the community. It takes decisions, evolves policies, prepares plans and allocates resources for all development activities. Yet development cannot be achieved. To achieve development, a catalyst action has to be performed by the Rural Institute. The New Panchayati Rai System has been established for which local body leaders and functionaries have to be trained and they are to be supported. As per the requirements of the Constitution of India, every district has to develop a development plan with the active participation of the people. As per the 14th Finance Commission recommendation and decision of the Ministry of Panchayati Raj, Government of India, every Gram Panchayat should prepare a participatory development plan which is called Gram Panchayat Development Plan (GPDP). It is mandatory on the part of the Gram panchayats to prepare plan to get the funds from the Central Government. For the preparation of the District Plan, and Gram Panchayat Development Plan, a planning machinery and a support structure are necessary. All development schemes which are implemented in the rural areas require awareness among the people for implementation. The needed awareness has to be created. The available rural skills have to be enhanced. The skills have to be linked productively with the market system. A new support system is needed for farmers to come out from the present crises. A strong emphasis on research and development is required to support SHGs and village and cottage industries. Having said the contextual problems before contextualising the whole framework of Rural University one has to bring to light what is exactly the Rural Institute or Rural University.

Rural University Framework

To get clarity on the concept of Rural University, one can go through the experience of the Visva Bharati University at Santiniketan. Dr. Ramachandran had explained the experience with adequate clarity.[26] It is not a mere transplantation of city education in a rural area. It is a deeper process of a synthesis of the rural background with the challenges of modern society. Visva Bharati University demonstrated the very natural ambience with simplicity and scientific living conditions along with artistic beauty. Students will be able to understand the beauty of nature and the rhythm and cadences of nature with human interactions only when they are allowed to live with nature. Students will have opportunity to go deeper into the nature and its dimensions in relation to human interaction. Tagore emphasized the great values of Truth, Beauty and Goodness embedded in the ancient rural culture. This hoary past has to be rediscovered and the values have to be renourished as part of the activities of a Rural University. Though he emphasized the rediscovery of the old values of the rural culture of India, he equally emphatically and asiduasouly argued in favour of synthesis between the good values of the old rural culture of India with the values of modern civilisation. The dominant thought that prevailed among the intellectuals, policy makers and administrators was in favour of the system which was introduced by the British Administration in India. Even at the dawn of Independence our leaders did not have the courage to introduce or to support the indigenous system of education. Even the intellectuals did not have the requisite argument to support the new system. It is only the Gandhian scholars lamented on the theme and did conduct some experiments. To portray the characteristics of a Rural University I rely on the observations of Dr. G. Ramachandran as he was instrumental in establishing Gandhigram Rural Institute. Being a Gandhian Scholar and a student of Rabindranath Tagore his observations about Rural University are basic and authentic.

Rural University should be founded on an ideology that establishes conviction on the assumption that there are certain materials, mental and spiritual values in the ancient rural civilisation and culture of India. The above values are to be discovered and renourished. It is to be made clear that this process do not contradicts the modern scientific and technological development values of the present day. One should understand the roots of the rural culture where one will find peacefulness as there was no competition for profit making exercise of individuals. The whole process of development is on cooperation for collective life either at the family life or at the community life. Cooperation adjustment, tolerances were with the attitude of the people in the rural areas.

Rural life is rooted in decentralisation of political and economic power and resources with the aim of reaching out to the maximum of people. In the whole process of rural development one will find deeper and functioning of artistry in the life of the people in the rural commodities. One should take note here that in the name of ruralising higher education it never reflects adoption of scientific and technological values in rural human life. Rural University takes higher education to the doorsteps of the people where they live closer to their occupation. The rural higher education is through the occupation of the people. It never keeps the people away from their occupation. It works on the improvement of the occupation through adoption of modern technology and scientific devices. Agriculture was the main basis of their occupation and hence the system of education is on agriculture primarily.

Further, the Rural Higher Education touches upon the allied activities of agriculture in the rural areas. They are village industries and handicrafts. It is woven around village industries and handicrafts. It should be not a big one as the urban centric university system. It should be optimum in size but its reach has to be extensive through the outreach programmes. Extension methods play crucial roles in this university system.

Rural University should be in a position to rely on own resource both human and material. Teachers and students should be engaged in production activities. Rural university will follow two language formula. One is mother tongue or regional language and Hindi, the national language. Any other language like English can be added. There should not be any subtraction from the two. Rural University unequivocally made it clear that it relies on local culture, practices, values and so on. India being culturally and spiritually rich and hence variations and diversities are abundant. Hence, they are to be accommodated. While producing students from Rural University, it strives to produce men and women as not as products to the market as job seekers. But, men and women will be prepared through proper orientation as an integrated personality to act as best citizens for the future. While orienting the students, the best spiritual traditions will be used. Rural University must revitalise the whole rural area where it is situated. Rural University campus will reflect the real transformation that takes place in the rural areas where the institute is located. Here one should register that even before the government took initiatives there should be experiments done by the non-governmental organisations. Whether they are recognised or not, they were also useful experiments. Having seen the characteristics of a Rural University one has to consider the new Rural University in the context of Globalisation.

Contextualisation

The whole exercise has to be done in the backdrop of Globalisation and the existing social and economic realities of rural India. Addressing those contextual rural problems is a tough task and that too through Gandhian framework is a challenging task.[27] The rural India has to be prepared to work towards social transformation by taking the advantages of globalisation and decentralisation and by avoiding the threats emanate from globalisation and decentralisation. Globalisation has brought newer technologies and free flow of resources. They can be profitably used by the rural masses for their advantages. The existing problems in the rural areas have to be tackled. The problems are: livelihood of the poor, production of the agricultural sector, poor maintenance of commons, large scale migration, poor health of the women and children, poor sanitation, poor water supply, poor conditions for primary schools, energy crisis. Apart from the above rural governance is yet another issue to be looked after.

Primarily World Class University with potential staff can address the above issues through the academic, research and outreach programmes. It has to produce a cadre of outstanding individuals from the new rural universities not to seek jobs but to create jobs and manage development in the rural areas.[28] Since Indian society has rich tradition, culture and civilisation it should have a strong knowledge base. Hence, they are to be explored, investigated. The new university has to work on the challenges of the rural society. By designing curriculum, offering programmes carrying out research all should be socially relevant. Rural University should be in policy advocacy front. In the same way it has to prepare qualified staff to rural development sector. It has to find out alternative approach of rural development which is sustainable in nature. It does not mean that it avoids globalisation opportunities. It makes use of globalisation opportunities and at the same time it avoids threats of globalisation.[29] Now, Nalanda University is in the formative stage which is going to concentrate on eastern knowledge.[30] It is to be noted that there is a general argument in India that educational system in India has not been concretely errected on Indian needs and ethos, which has ultimately affected the whole fabric of the Indian society.[31] In this context, the proposed Nalanda University and the Rural Universities will be of immense use to evolve a meaningful system of education in line with culture and ethos of India.

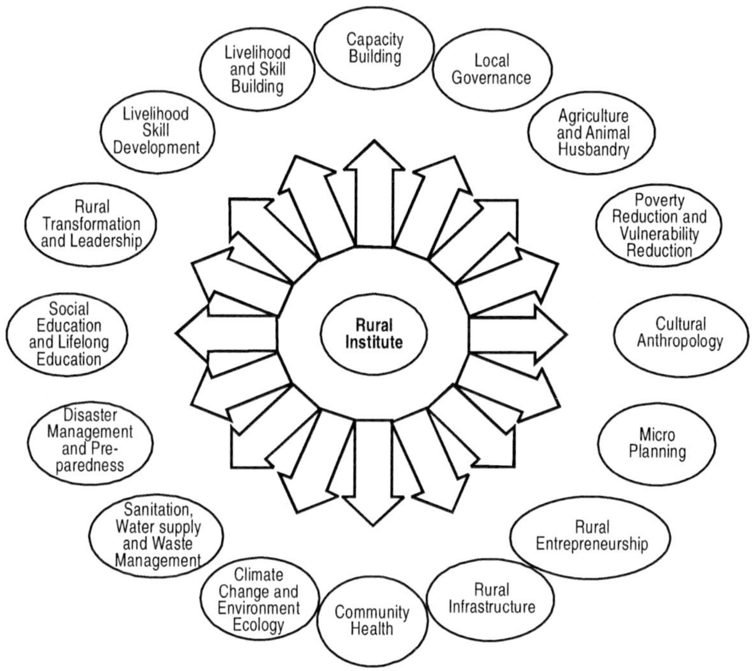

Fig.: Rural Institute in a New Context

It should have a slim structure and delivery point should be broader. It need not follow the existing pattern of traditional universities. It has to extend Research and Development (R&D) support to all rural development activities. Be it self-help group or agriculture or small scale industries or sanitation or water supply or traditional health practices or waste management, natural resource management, or energy from alternative source, or upgradation of rural skills, or enhancement of rural technology or rural governance or micro level planning, all can get the needed support from the Rural University. The new rural university will not be in comfort zone but it will be working on the challenges thrown by the rural communities. It not only creates cadres for rural development it will also train, orient the existing staff of rural development departments. Further, it will build the capacity of the elected representatives of the local bodies. It will have effective linkage with rural communities, rural organisations and institutions. It should emerge as support institution for the rural communities and the government for effective management of rural development programmes. The new rural university will have a social audit system for its functions. Its impact on the society will be evaluated every five years by fixing certain observable indictors. The existing rural universities can be taken away from the UGC and put it under the NCRI. The funds have to be routed through the NCRI. The rural institutes need not follow the conventional Universities. It can develop its own pattern as the Indian Institute of Management, Ahmedabad.

Conclusion

'Rural University' has its own history in India since 1948. Yet concretely one cannot say that the Rural University has emerged as a matured educational system in India. Ever since it was recognised as a system of education in India from the dawn of Independence efforts were on to conceptualise and reconceptualise rural higher education and yet government had not fully committed to extend support to this system of education. Yet, the institutions created in the nomenclature have delivered goods and services more than the traditional higher educational institutions modelled on the West. The Rural Institutes had been functioning with lot of systemic barriers and challenges. The challenges have not been faced and responded as it requires teachers with extraordinary adventurism. Rural higher education has to move in an adventuristic path. It needs extraordinary teachers and students. But, the barriers are system related and imposed by the funding agencies. But context warrants such a kind of rural higher education today to address the emerging issues in the rural areas. In all the times government provided only token approvals and not extended full-fledged committed support. All the experiments have not yielded the expected results but they have indicated the potentials of such education. Most of the Rural Institutes joined the mainstream not because of the failure of the education system, but, because of the poor support extended to this new experiment by the government. The rural areas are facing civilisational environmental and ecological crises today. Mainstream education do not have wherewithal to address the rural crises. The farming communities, craft communities, marginalised, fishing folks, tribal communities are in deep trouble. The problems faced by the rural rustic folk have been intensified by the economic globalisation activities. Environment and ecology are in deep crises. Hence, a new rural university system has to be established to respond to the challenges of the rural society due to the impact of globalisation. The new rural university system is need based, contextual, outreach and advocacy oriented. The new system should have manageable structure and delivery points. Extension and social audit system will be in place in the new rural university system. This new Rural Institute can be created within the framework of Institute of excellence of the Government of India.

Notes and References

1. G. Palanithurai and R. Ramesh (2008), *Globalisation: Issues at Grassroots*. New Delhi: Concept Publishing Company Pvt. Ltd.; G. Palanithurai and R. Ramesh, (2010), *Globalisation and Rural Development*. New Delhi: Concept Publishing Company Pvt. Ltd.
2. The World Bank (2004), *Fiscal Decentralisation to Rural Governments in India*, New Delhi: Oxford University Press.
3. P.V. Narasimha Rao (1995), *Rural Universities: My Vision*. Inaugural Address. Hyderabad: National Council of Rural Institutes.
4. The nomenclatures 'Rural Institute' and 'Rural University' have been used interchangeably by the scholars in their writings. But a few make distinction. Rural university is considered as an apex institution.
5. G. Palanithurai (2012), *Social Relevance of Higher Learning Institutions*. New Delhi: Concept Publishing Company Pvt. Ltd., pp. 99-121.

6. NCRI, Directory of Rural Institutes. New Delhi: Serials Publications, 2010.
7. Convocation Address by R. Venkataraman, P.V. Narasimha Rao, G. Ramachandran, M.S. Swaminathan, C. Subramanian, A.T. Ariyaratne and L.C. Jain, Gandhigram Rural Institute, *Convocation Addresses* (Gandhigram: Gandhigram Rural Institute, 2002).
8. T. Karunakaran and Regi Thomas (2012), *Liberating Education for a Knowledge Society.* Sevagram: Nai-Talim Samiti Publications.
9. K.C.R. Raja (ed.) (1964). *Thoughts and Talks of G. Ramachandran*, Gandhigram: Gandhigram Publications, pp. 310–312.
10. In the Communication of Government of India, Ministry of Education, No. 55-5/47-3/3 dated 4th November, 1948, there was no mention of rural university, but in the section (IX) in the terms of reference, there was a mention of the need for more universities on a regional or other bases. Taking the cue from the above, a separate section was written.
11. Arun Kumar Dave (2009), "A Rural University – Need of the Nation", *Ailaan,* Vol. II, No. 11 (February).
12. Since Rural India had its own livelihood, culture, trade, skills, crafts and so on for 80 per cent of the population, the author of the chapter in the Radhakrishnan Commission wanted to bring about transformation and reconstruction keeping the core values of India in focus and for this he suggested a new framework of education for rural development. Further, the whole edifice of the framework has to be anchored on the concept of '*Nai Talim*'. As per this chapter, the expansion of higher education should have been on this framework. But, unfortunately, it did not take place. Later, there were different versions of the need for Rural Universities. One set of arguments is that it has to educate the rural masses formally and informally. Another set of arguments is that this university has to have live linkages with communities. It has to conduct outreach programmes. Yet, another argument is projected about the role of rural university: it has to extend ideas, information, technology, skill, and capacity and so on, to the rural communities through its outreach programmes and students learn by doing such activities. There is one more argument that it has to do research on rural development

issues and help the community and the government to achieve the target of their activities.

13. Gandhigram Rural Institute, *Experts from NAAC Peer-Team Report.* (Gandhigram, Circular dated 13th October, 2016).
14. For details see graduate attributes in the website of the Gandhigram Rural Institute. www.ruraluniv.ac.in
15. Recently Mr. S.M. Vijayanand, Former Secretary, Ministry of Panchayati Raj, Government of India, Former Chief Secretary, Government of Kerala and a practicing Gandhian has been invited to interact with the faculty members on "how to reinvent Rural Institute". The programme held on 31st August, 2017 and the entire speech is in the institute website. www.ruraluniv.ac.in
16. Samir Banerjee (2009), *Notes from Gandhigram: Challenges to Gandhian Praxis.* Hyderabad: Orient Blackswan.
17. National Council of Rural Institute, *A New Dawn on Rural Higher Education from Chaos to Order*, Hyderabad: National Council of Rural Institutes, 2001.
18. P.V. Narasimha Rao, 1995, *op. cit.*
19. S.V. Prabhath (2010), *Perspectives on Nai Talim.* New Delhi: Serials Publications.
20. Ram Takwale (2009), "*Nai Talim* of Connected Society with Education for Transformation" *Ailaan,* (Vol. II: No. 1 January).
21. With the support of the Ford Foundation, serious studies have been conducted on the implications of globalisation and as a result a newsletter is being circulated among the panchayats entitled *Global and Local.*
22. World Bank (2009), *Reshaping Economic Geography: World Development Report,* 2009. Washington, DC: The World Bank.
23. Budd Hall, Rajesh Tandon and Crystal Trenblay (eds.) (2015), *Strengthening Community University Research Partnerships: Global Perspectives.* (British Columbia: University of Victoria); Rajesh Tandon, Budd Hall, Walter Lepore and Wafa Singh (eds.) (2016), *Knowledge and Engagement: Building Capacity for the Next Generation of Community based Researchers.* New Delhi: PRIA Publications.

24. V. Padmanabhan (1996), *Grammar for Rural Development.* Madurai: Khadi Friends Forum.
25. V. Padmanabhan, (1997), *Gandhigram Golden Jubilee: 1947-1997.* Gandhigram: Gandhigram Trust.
26. Dr. G. Ramachandran had explained in one of his lectures the characteristics of a Rural University for more details refer part Four, Seventh Chapter in K.C.R. Raja (ed.) *Thoughts and Talks of G. Ramachandran* (Gandhigram: Gandhigram Publications, 1964, pp. 310-317.
27. Samir Banerjee, 2009, *op. cit.*
28. G. Palanithurai, (2017), "Where are World Class Rural Institutes?" *Millennium Post*. 19th January, New Delhi.
29. Gandhigram Rural Institute has prepared a blue print for making it as a Central Rural University and it is being submitted to the Government of India. For more details see Gandhigram Rural University, *Proposal for Gandhigram Central Rural University* (Gandhigram: University Publication, 2006).
30. S.D. Muni (2010), "Nalanda: a soft power project", *The Hindu*, 31st August.
31. K.N. Panikkar (2009). "Towards a New Paradigms in Education", *The Hindu* (9 May) p. 12.

■ ■ ■

2

Vision for a National Rural University

V. Ragupathy

Withering Indian Villages and the Crisis at the Grassroots—Challenge to the Intellectual and Scientific Community

The colossal challenge to India at the moment is the boiling crises at the grassroots. Indian villages are virtually facing the danger of extinction today in terms of its livelihood, values, culture and its original civilisation roots. Still we are in a position to debate over the observations of B.R. Ambedkar and M.K. Gandhi. The intellectual and scientific community is not able to adequately and forcefully address those vital issues of rural India. Because of varied reasons 745 universities, 40,000 colleges and 11,000 research institutions in India[1] somehow are untouched by the sufferings of rural India. The academic and research priorities of our higher learning institutions are different. Based on the needs of the market and the industries mostly they prepare human resources to serve in urban areas. Villages are not in their priority. In such a way our educational system, process and practices have been developed. Occasionally, these issues have been discussed and decisions had been taken to pluck the loopholes and yet, the mainstream education focuses its attention only on industrial needs, service needs, and market needs but not the needs[2] of the rural population. Occasionally the conventional universities introduced academic programmes on rural development to prepare manpower for rural development sector.

But, in reality the rural and agrarian crises may soon emerge as an enormous assault to the foundations of the polity and the economy of the nation. It may emerge as a destabiliser of the nation if it is not scientifically understood and addressed quickly and professionally. Agro-pastoral system of the Indian villages is now under severe stress. The swelling Indian agrarian crisis is directly related to the environmental dilapidation of India at the grassroots. It is a pointer that the foundation of India is withering away. The rural indebtedness, farmer's suicide and abject poverty are nothing but the result of an economy of rural marginalisation. The self-reliant natures of Indian villages have been systematically eroded and the villages have been weakened. Millions of villagers are disempowered and driven to dependency syndrome for their basic needs. The deep-rooted self-esteem and self-confidence of the farmers and rural craftsmen have been thoroughly mantled. The proud farming community now stands weak, helpless and fragile. The villages of India are the roots of India and the grandiose nation survives on these roots. If the villages perish, the grandiose nation will perish. The brittled villages of India are the markers of a brittled nation.

Indian villages give the foundation for the cultural identity of the nation. The culture of India is embedded in the cultural strength of our villages. The communities at the grassroots cherish the endangered cultural heritage of India in its various forms and shades. But, the cultural identity and characteristic of villages of India are passing through an existential dilemma. The cultural heritage of Indian villages is withering away in recent years and it may result in the withering away of the cultural foundation and identity of the nation.

Even though Indian villages are the lifeline of the nation, they are subjugated colonial masters and subsequently by the massive industrial and market economy activities. Villages are considered as the source and supplier of raw materials at a discounted price during the British Raj and the same conditions continued in different form at present. The market economy has developed a very efficient system to devalue the rural produces. There is inadequate scientific investigation of such burning issues by the scientific community. Indian village communities are the custodian and guardian of our natural resources. Farming communities, pastoral communities, craft communities, tribal communities and fishing communities are protecting and sustaining our land, water bodies, forest, pastoral lands, and coastal areas. These communities protect our rich cultural heritages. Rural communities protect our traditions and our unique national identity. These are the real wealth of our nation. Spiritual and cultural affluence has not been valued and respected. Rural communities protect this wealth without expecting any incentive from the nation. It is a way of life and part of their culture and tradition. Some of such national traditions as old as our *Itihasas* are still conserved and enriched by our village communities. Still everything related to the villages is devalued, belittled and marginalised. The sublime suppression of the local rural India has deep effects on their existence. Villages do not give many opportunities for the youth for their progress and it results in the alienation of youth from the rural community. The anti-national forces are able to exploit the helplessness of the poor at the grassroots and it facilitates the emergence of militancy and terrorism in many of the states. One-third of India is disturbed because of the extremist elements.

Indian villages stand for the lofty Indian values. Hard work, nurturing, culturing, saving, preserving perseverance, sharing, caring, mutuality, frugality, simplicity, and others are the core values of the life in the villages. The village is a system closely connected to the ecology. The core values of *Vedas*, *Upanishads*, *Itihasas* are still kept alive in the culture of our villages.[3] Great Indian leaders like Tilak, Tagore, Aurobindo, and Gandhi struggled for the rejuvenation of Indian villages. During Indian National Movement and Freedom Struggle rebuilding India on the rich village values was a common vision of many of our national leaders. It was considered as an integral part of nation building process.

National Movement and Renaissance of Rural India

National movement had a dream of regenerating the rich heritage of Indian village system. It was an essential objective of our freedom struggle. This could be traced in the writings of leaders like Tilak,

Tagore[4], Aurobindo[5], Gandhi[6] and Patel. Village was considered as the symbol of India. Gurudev Rabindranath Tagore started Sriniketan as a pioneer model for the regeneration of Indian villages[7]. Gurudev wanted to regenerate Indian villages as they were the treasure houses of Indian arts and culture. Gandhi gave the concept of *Gram Swaraj* as a means to achieve the true national freedom. He believed that without attaining the fullest *Swaraj* of people at the villages, National *Swaraj* could not be achieved in the real sense. To him only by achieving village *swaraj* people at the grassroots could be liberated. He wanted to promote national institutions of higher education for this purpose. He founded Gujarat Vidyapeeth, Kasi Vidyapeeth and many other institutions to take these Ideas forward. During the freedom movement Gandhiji started many initiatives to create centres for science and technology for the promotion of the livelihood needs of the poor at the grassroots. He founded All India Village Industries Association and eminent scientists and intellectuals like Sir C.V. Raman, Sir Jagadish Chandra Bose and Dr. B.C. Roy were the members of the advisory committee of the association. In the post-Independence era, these ideas have been shaped and strengthened by great leaders like Acharya Kripalani, Jayaprakash Narayan[8], Rammanohar Lohia[9] and Deendayal Upadhyay.[10] Jayaprakash Narayan wanted a total revolution steering from the villages of India. Deendayal Upadhyay in his theory of integral humanism vehemently argued for building modern India on the vibrant villages. He believed that the economy and polity of the nation largely depend on the vitality of the villages at the foundation.

But the post-independent India depended largely on a centralised model of development in which importance and primacy were given to industrialisation.[11] As a result, rural economy was relegated to the background. Our educational system largely contributed for the growth of industries, urbanisation and expansion of government machinery. In this context, our government[12] gave a secondary status to villages in the development process. Initiatives taken by the government at the dawn of Independence to develop the rural areas through series of programmes from community development to integrate rural development, have achieved only some physical targets neglecting the community.[12] Systematic failures have been captured by the scholars and as a result community driven development approach and particularly development gained currency among the practitioners of development.[13] The trickle down model of the post-independent era trickled down invariably misery and poverty. India cannot survive as a nation, if its villages fall apart. India's development will be an illusion if its villages are fractured. To regenerate Indian villages, a massive national intellectual initiative of scientists, social scientists, management experts and artist is required. In the initial years of independence initiatives were made to promote few rural institutes in some states of India. This experiment made significant progress and rural institutes produced an army of capacitated and dedicated youth in the field of rural development. They formed the core human resource for the historical community development programme of the nation. They did outstanding services in the fields of rural development social welfare, women and child development. They immensely contributed for the growth of NGO movement in south India. Some of them made outstanding contributions to the nation in different areas like art-culture and literature. Gandhigram Rural Institute founded in 1956 was one of such an experiment and based on its outstanding contributions Government of India gave the deemed university status in 1976.[14] Gandhigram Rural Institute has emerged successfully as a functional institute. But, the rural institute model was not able to get the required support from the government and all the other rural institutes were closed. Dr. Nanaji Deshmukh initiated a bold experiment on Rural University in Chitrakoot. Mahatma Gandhi Rural University founded by him was first of its kind and because of his leadership and commitment it has made significant progress. Acharya N.G. Ranga Rural University started in Andhra Pradesh is struggling hard to achieve its objectives. Such initiative need full support from the UGC and Ministry of Human Resource

Development, Rural Development, Panchayati Raj, Agriculture and Small and Medium and Cottage Industries. Some of the standard policies of government and UGC are not encouraging such innovative academic institutions. Such innovative institution must have more freedom and autonomy and they may not be forced to follow the standard framework uniformly prescribed. Dr. Abdul Kalam and many other great scientists and technologist attempted to give a science and technology framework for regenerating Indian villages. PURA model of Kalam attracted few of the universities and Kalam could generate interest among scientific community in rural development. But such sporadic and periodic initiatives could not generate long-lasting results. Science and technology, particularly sustainable technologies are critically required for the regeneration of Indian villages. Completely different approaches and frameworks in social sciences, particularly in politics and economics are required for this task. Management science has a major share in the formidable work of regeneration of Indian villages in the context of globalisation.

Building Prosperous Smart Villages: Agenda for the Nation

Today India needs a new generation of knowledge enriched smart villages. Enormous intellectual scientific managerial and technological inputs are required to develop smart villages. The smart villages must be self-supporting eco-friendly and self-governing little republics. Only such smart villages can ensure real prosperity based on enriched ecosystem and enriched social system. Gandhiji wanted Indian villages to blossom into Eden Gardens. His picture of the village is indeed a picture of an ideal smart village. Villages can be recreated restructured remodeled and repositioned. New modern self-sufficient villages can replace the old depleted and under developed villages. The ecology of the villages can be restored and the richness of the rural environment can regenerate villages which mean nothing but the regeneration of the land, the water bodies, the forests and other natural wealth of India. The ecological wealth of India can be rebuilt only by rebuilding village Eco systems. Variety of micro crafts, small and medium enterprises to suit the contemporary requirements must be nurtured. There are unlimited opportunities for rural start-ups in the fields like water, sanitation, health, education, agro-industries, and rural health. It can generate not only full employment, but also can eradicate rural poverty. Digitalising villages can bring most of the facilities and services to the doorsteps of the villagers and ensure efficiency of their delivery. E-Governance is an area which can bring transparency, quality, responsiveness and accountability in grassroots governance.

Vision for a National Rural University

The scientific and intellectual communities in India today are not seriously and adequately focusing their work on the problems affecting Indian villages today. India needs an army of committed intellectuals and scientists to work for the prosperity of Indian villages. Intellectual and scientific community of the nation has accountability and responsibility of giving back to the people at the villages of India. Government of India now wants to give more focus on the problems of the people at the grassroots. The problems at the grassroots are highly complex in nature and they require constant scientific investigation. Some of the best intellectuals and scientists of the nation must be specifically engaged constantly to analyse the issues at the grassroots and search for answers and solutions. They require freedom and autonomy for ensuring a high level of objective intellectual exploration. This process must be institutionalised.

To achieve this mission India needs a National Rural University as a special purpose vehicle to serve the needs of villages of India. India has Central and State Universities. Most of these universities have their roots from the colonial British educational philosophy. Indian universities are much influenced by the concepts, ideas and frameworks borrowed from the West. They do not have their roots in the Indian soil. They are not much sensitive to the realities at the grassroots. The universities are mostly promoting urban values, viewpoints and frameworks. Their interest in rural India is very marginal. More often they ignore the marginal sections of Indian, villages, like farmers, dalits, tribal, craftsman, fishermen and many others.

In this context a National Rural University (NRU) must be promoted as an innovative and alternative model in higher education. It will be rooted on the cultural ethos and values of the village India. It will reflect on the issues of the Indian villages and take them to the national attention. The National Rural University will develop a strong network of intellectuals, academics, activists, policy makers and the villagers. It will highlight the pains and problems of the villagers. It will design new ways and strategies to solve the problem of the Indian villages. The National Rural University will be a national think tank for the villages of India. It will capture the ideas, strategies and solution through discourse and deliberation. The university will see the national issues from the perspective of the village communities. It will serve as a national observatory for capturing the ground level realities. National Rural University will provide platform for national level debates and discourses and facilitate brain storming on the issues of the people at the grassroots. It will give the podium for the villagers to articulate their views to the nation. National Rural University will be a centre for the regeneration of the endangered values and ethos of the rich rural life. It will bring back the glory, brilliance and beauty of rural India.

Objectives of National Rural University

The National Rural University will have the following objectives:

1. It will serve as a special purpose vehicle to provide Intellectual, Scientific, Technological, Managerial, and Policy inputs required for the creation of sustainable self-reliant smart villages.

2. It will develop academic programmes for preparing human resources required to work for the sustainable and integral rural development.
3. It will rediscover and promote the endangered art-culture and values and heritage of rural India.
4. It will promote research in science technology humanities on themes related to rural regeneration and transformation.
5. It will develop academics with strong commitment to use their knowledge and capacity to serve the marginalised communities in the rural India.
6. It will incubate and promote innovative and replicable outreach models of sustainable rural development to be experimented in the field and to be shared with other institutions and agencies.
7. It will incubate rural start-ups and promote innovative industrial and business ventures at the grassroots.
8. It will provide a platform for free intellectual debates, discourses, and deliberations on rural issues.
9. It will provide a podium for the marginalised and excluded groups to express their views opinions and ideas related to their livelihood to the nation.
10. It will serve as an observatory of the status of the villages and provide reliable empirical data and inputs to the stakeholders.
11. It will give policy inputs to Central and State Governments and other development agencies.

Innovation in Education

National Rural University (NRU) will develop an appropriate model of education to achieve its objectives. It will introduce innovations in teaching research and outreach programmes. It will have unique academic programmes based on sandwich model to give opportunities to students to learn by practical application of knowledge in the field. Academic programme will have more focus on application of knowledge skill and technology in the field. Students will be encouraged to develop individual and group real life models of development at the grassroots. NRU will have partnership with village panchayats, women self-help groups, community based organisations, NGOs, civil society, media, industry, business institutions and NRI groups. NRU will have training institutions to conduct training programmes to personnel's who are in rural development sector. It will have a separate leadership school to prepare rural transformational leaders for the rural and urban local body institutions.

Structure and Function of National Rural University

National Rural University will be a centrally sponsored institution of national importance. It will be a special purpose vehicle to do research on rural issues. It will enjoy full academic and functional autonomy. Government and UGC will allow NRU to pursue path-breaking endeavours, ventures, experiments, and innovations. It should provide enormous opportunities for the passionate and committed individuals and groups to work in the university with their own resources and knowledge both from within India and abroad for rural transformation. Flexible regulations have to be evolved to involve bilateral and multilateral organisations to work for rural transformation. NRU will be accountable for its functioning and performance. It will ensure measurable outputs and outcomes. It may be enabled to evolve several models through experiments for replication. It will function through faculties closely connected with the livelihood of people at the grassroots. It will have focus on application aspects. It will use state of art tools to achieve its objectives. It will have linkages with international, national and state level rural development institutions. It should have linkages with rural communities through outreach programmes. The university will have unconventional and unique wings and practices to work for rural transformation and sustainable development. National Rural University will have the pluralistic character to accommodate the diversity of Indian villages. It will have multidisciplinary and interdisciplinary centres of excellence. National university must configure the best brains, the best technology and the best management systems for the development of the villages. National Rural University will be an independent monitoring system of policies, programmes, procedures affecting the villages of India. It will also monitor the market system affecting the villages and capture the issues affecting the villages. It will promote the state-of-art, science and technology for the development of the villages.

It will also promote the rural arts, crafts and cultures. The National Rural University will be the centre of inter-university excellence. It will promote similar programmes and activities in other regular universities and colleges. The National Rural University must be an All India Institution and it must be a national platform for collaborative ventures. Ministries of Rural Development, Agriculture, Water Resources, Industry, Science and Technology, Health, Culture and many others must be the partners of this initiative. NRU will provide enormous opportunities to passionate youth to work in this mission without any restriction. Young minds who have passion and commitment to work for new rural India can work in this university. They will work for short time, long term and in projects. This university pay and allowances are determined on the basis of output and outcome. Varied streams of pay will be in operation in this university. All the centres are autonomous centres and the functioning will be facilitated by a team at the university president's office. No conventional designations like Dean, Professor, Associate Professor, and Assistant Professor will be in this university. All will be designated as faculty level I, II and III. Anyone will coordinate the activities in the centre from among the faculty members. It will be free from designations and hierarchies. Absolutely it will be freed from the clutches of the bureaucracy. High moral and ethical standards will be evolved for functioning of the staff of this university. Ethical values will be given primacy in this university for its functioning. This university will have faculties with passion and sense of commitment towards the creation of a new rural India. The president of India must be the visitor and Prime Minister must be the chancellor of the National Rural University. NRU will have a slim governance structure and simple process and procedures. The university will give support to the government in formulating and executing the policies for rural development.

Conclusion

India, in the waves of globalisation and liberalisation is in the danger of losing some of its unique and sacred identities values and heritages. Indian villages are the most sacred identity of India. They give livelihood to two-third of the Indians. Indian villages are the guardians, custodians and forces defending the ecological wealth of the nation. India cannot achieve real prosperity and development when lakhs of its villages are withering and vanishing. Intellectual and scientific community must be facilitated to address these vital problems of the nation through the creation of a new National Rural University (NRU). India needs constant independent and scientific monitoring and investigation of rural issues and objective policy formulation. In this backdrop India needs a new National Rural University. The new National Rural University will help evolving appropriate policies, strategies and technologies to bring life and energy to the Indian village system. It will help to synthesize the values of our rural heritage with the vision of the nation for the future. It will help the nation to regenerate millions of villages of India and take sustainable development to the doorsteps of eight hundred million Indians living in the villages of India. The new National Rural University will shoulder the responsibility of transforming rural India with Central and State Governments.

Notes and References

1. UGC (2007). *A Brief Report of the National Conference on Development of Higher Education.* New Delhi: University Grant Commission (UGC).
2. Rajesh Tandon, Budd Hall, Walter Lepore and Wafa Singh (eds.) (2016). *Knowledge and Engagement: Building Capacity for the Next Generation of Community based Researchers*. New Delhi: PRIA.
3. Saletor, B.A. (1968) *Ancient Indian Political Thought.* Asia Publishing House, Bombay, pp. 74-75.
4. Sudhir Sen (1943), *Rabindranath Tagore on Rural Reconstruction,* Cornell University, Visva Bharati.
5. Vishwanath Prasad Varma (1990). *The Political Philosophy of Sri Aurobindo*, Delhi: Motilal Banarsidass Publication.
6. G. Palanithurai (2012). *Social Relevance of Higher Learning Institutions*. New Delhi: Concept Publishing Company Pvt. Ltd.
7. J.C. Kumarappa (1946). *Why the Village Movement?* Wardha: The All India Village Industries Association.
8. Asha Sinha (1997). *Political Philosophy of Jayaprakash Narayan.* University of Michigan: Janaki Prakashan.
9. Haribhau Limaye (2001). *Dr. Rammanohar Lohia: Battles for Liberty and Justice*. Rammanohar Lohia Smrutikendra, Sadashiv Bagaitkar Smrutimala.
10. Deendayal Upadhyay (1980). *Integral Humanism An Analysis of Some Basic Elements*, Prabhat Prakashan.
11. Arvind Virmani (2002). New Development Paradigm: Employment, Entitlement and Empowerment. *Economic and Political Weekly*, 1st June, pp. 2151-2160.
12. Robert Chamber (1996). *Putting the Last First*. London: Zed Books.
13. World Bank (2001). *CDD Approach for Development*. Washington DC: The World Bank.
14. G. Palanithurai (2012). *Village Development through Gandhian Framework* (in Tamil). Madurai: Tamil Nadu Sarvodaya Mandal.

Plea

This monograph is written not with an intension of adding one more publication in my CV. Ever since I joined the Gandhigram Rural Institute I keenly observed the functioning of the institute. It is visible that the institute has grown structurally and functionally. Outlays and outputs have been increased enormously. If its functions and performances are compared with the conventional universities, its performance is second to none. But it deviates from its basic objectives. Repeatedly I have been taking efforts to contextualise the institute to cater to the needs of the rural areas in the backdrop of the objectives fixed by the founders of the institute at a limited level. At one point of time when Dr. T. Karunakaran was the Vice-Chancellor we took earnest effort to prepare a proposal to make it as a central rural university. It was prepared with the intension of facing the effects of economic globalisation. Former President of India Dr. A.P.J. Abdul Kalam visited our institute and made a fervent plea that this university should be made as a Central University and it should work for rural transformation by keeping the basic objectives fixed by the founders of the institute. Based on his plea we prepared a proposal and presented before the Member of Parliament of Tamil Nadu in Tamil Nadu Bhavan, New Delhi. In fact the Members of Parliament who attended the meeting unanimously agreed to support this demand. In the meanwhile, there was a letter from the Central Government to State Government asking clearance for elevating the rural institute into a Central University. It was informed that the State Government wrote a letter replying to the letter that let the Gandhigram Rural Institute work for rural transformation in the same level as deemed to be university. This letter was written in the context of sanctioning one Central

University to Tamil Nadu. At this juncture, there was a fear that if the Gandhigram Rural Institute is elevated to the level of Central University, the proposal of setting up of a Central University at Thiruvarur will be dropped. I have argued with many that Tamil Nadu will get two such Central Universities as other States. It needs only an amendment in the existing rules. If Central Government wants to set up one more Central University, it can do it. Now, we are making a plea to create one more Central Rural University not because of celebrating the 150th year of M.K. Gandhi's birth anniversary but to solve the rural crises. This has to be considered in perspective. In India, 350 million people live in absolute poverty. Government of India affirms that 30 per cent of the people in India are poor. These people survive with Rs. 26 per day per person in the rural areas. It is also estimate that 65 million people have been displaced due to development projects. Nearly 680 million Indians cannot meet their basic needs. 40 per cent to 60 per cent of the population lacks accuses to basic entitlements such as health care, drinking water and sanitation. Of the total population 68 per cent of them are in the rural areas. They include: forming community, pastoral community, tribal community, fishing community and craft community. Their conditions are worsening day by day. Rural environment and ecological conditions are also getting deteriorated. Unless these communities are enabled through knowledge, skill, science and technology, they cannot lead a decent dignified human life. It is possible only through the creation of a new higher learning institution to connect with community through its outreach activities.

Rural communities are to be assisted to restore their livelihood. They need knowledge, skill, guidance, to improve their quality and standard of life. Against this background, we are making a fervent plea that either to upgrade this Gandhigram Rural Institute to the level of a Central University or to create a National Rural University. It should be done in an innovative way. It should be autonomous with the liberal funding and support of both Government and private agencies. It should take up socially relevant issues for research, offer socially relevant courses and continuously work with communities. The survival and sustainability of the institute depends on its performance. Its survival relies on the support of the people and stakeholders. There are many universities in China working with communities and rural production centres. In the same way, the New Rural National University has to work with communities and rural production centres. Apart from the above a new rural education policy has to be evolved with a perspective of preparing human power for rural transformation.

■ ■ ■

Bibliography

Banerjee, Samir (2009). *Notes from Gandhigram: Challenges to Gandhian Praxis*. Hyderabad: Orient Blackswan.

Dave, Arun Kumar (2009), "A Rural University – Need of the Nation" *Ailaan*, Vol. II, No. 11, February.

Gandhigram Rural Institute (2002), *Convocation Addresses*. Gandhigram: Gandhigram Rural Institute.

Gandhigram Rural Institute (2016), *Experts from NAAC Peer-Team Report*. Gandhigram.

Gandhigram Rural University (2006), *Proposal for Gandhigram Central Rural University*, Gandhigram: University Publication.

Hall, Budd, Tandon Rajesh and Trenblay Crystal (2015) (eds.) *Strengthening Community University Research Partnerships: Global Perspectives*. British Columbia: University of Victoria; Tandon, Rajesh, Hall, Budd, Lepore Walter and Singh Wafa (2016) (eds.) *Knowledge and Engagement: Building Capacity for the Next Generation of Community based Researchers*. New Delhi: PRIA Publications.

Karunakaran, T. and Thomas Regi (2012), *Liberating Education for a Knowledge Society*. Sevagram: Nai-Thalim Samiti Publications.

Kumarappa, J.C. (1946). *Why the Village Movement?* Wardha: The All India Village Industries Association.

Limaye, Haribhau (2001). *Dr. Rammanohar Lohia: Battles for Liberty and Justice*. Rammanohar Lohia Smrutikendra, Sadashiv Bagaitkar Smrutimala.

Muni, S.D. (2010), "Nalanda: A Soft Power Project", *The Hindu*, 31st August.

Narasimha Rao, P.V. (1995), "*Rural Universities: My Vision*". Inaugural Address. Hyderabad: National Council of Rural Institutes.

National Council of Rural Institute (2001), *A New Dawn on Rural Higher Education from Chaos to Order*. Hyderabad: National Council of Rural Institutes.

NCRI (2010), *Directory of Rural Institutes*. New Delhi: Serials Publications.

Padmanabhan, V. (1996), *Grammar for Rural Development*. Madurai: Khadi Friends Forum.

Padmanabhan, V. (1997), *Gandhigram Golden Jubilee: 1947-1997*. Gandhigram: Gandhigram Trust.

Palanithurai, G. (2012), *Social Relevance of Higher Learning Institutions*. New Delhi: Concept Publishing Company (P) Ltd., pp. 99-121.

Palanithurai, G. (2012). *Village Development through Gandhian Framework* (in Tamil). Madurai: Tamil Nadu Sarvodaya Mandal.

Palanithurai, G. (2017) "Where are World Class Rural Institutes?" *Millennium Post*, 19th January, New Delhi.

Palanithurai, G. and Ramesh, R. (2008), *Globalisation: Issues at Grassroots*. New Delhi: Concept Publishing Company; Palanithurai, G. and Ramesh, R. (2010), *Globalisation and Rural Development*. New Delhi: Concept Publishing Company Pvt. Ltd.

Panikkar, K.N. (2009), "Towards a New Paradigms in Education", *The Hindu*, 9 May, p. 12.

Prabhath, S.V. (2010), *Perspectives on Nai-Talim*. New Delhi: Serials Publications.

Raja, K.C.R. (1964) (ed.) *Thoughts and Talks of G. Ramachandran*, Gandhigram: Gandhigram Publications.

Saletor, B.A. (1968) *Ancient Indian Political Thought*. Bombay: Asia Publishing House, pp. 74-75.

Sen, Sudhir (1943), *Rabindranath Tagore on Rural Reconstruction*, Cornell University: Visva-Bharati.

Sinha, Asha (1997) *Political Philosophy of Jayaprakash Narayan*. University of Michigan: Janaki Prakashan.

Takwale, Ram (2009) "Nai Talim of Connected Society with Education for Transformation", *Ailaan*, Vol II, No. 1, January.

Tandon, Rajesh, Hall, Budd, Lepore, Walter and Singh: Wafa (eds.) (2016). *Knowledge and Engagement: Building Capacity for the Next Generation of Community based Researchers*. New Delhi: PRIA.

The World Bank (2001). *CDD Approach for Development*. Washington DC: The World Bank.

The World Bank (2004), *Fiscal Decentralisation to Rural Governments in India*, New Delhi: Oxford University Press.

The World Bank (2009), *Reshaping Economic Geography: World Development Report, 2009*. Washington, DC: The World Bank.

UGC (2007). *A Brief Report of the National Conference on Development of Higher Education.* New Delhi: University Grant Commission (UGC).

Upadhyay, Deendayal (1969). *Integral Humanism: An Analysis of Some Basic Elements*, Prabhat Prakashan.

Varma, Vishwanath Prasad (1990). *The Political Philosophy of Sri Aurobindo*, Delhi: Motilal Banarsidass Publication.

Virmani, Arvind (2002). "New Development Paradigm: Employment, Entitlement and Empowerment. *Economic and Political Weekly.* 1st June, pp. 2151-2160; Chamber, Robert (1996). *Putting the Last First*. London: Zed Books.

Index